C
929.92 SON
Sonneborn, Liz.
The star-spangled banner :
the story behind our nation
CC 1067764900   FEB   2006

D1442493

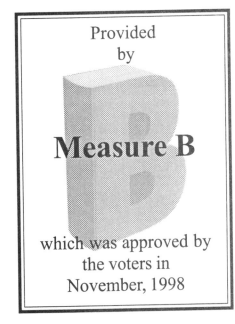

Provided
by

Measure B

which was approved by
the voters in
November, 1998

The Star-Spangled Banner

The Story Behind Our National Anthem

THE GOOD OLD FLAG.

THE

STAR SPANGLED BANNER.

SOLO AND CHORUS.

PUBLISHED BY

HEATH, WYNKOOP & CO.,

PERFUMERS

No. 63 LIBERTY STREET, NEW YORK

1861.

Liz Sonneborn

CHELSEA
CLUBHOUSE

An Imprint of Chelsea House Publishers

A Haights Cross Communications Company

Philadelphia

Chelsea Clubhouse books are published by Chelsea House Publishers, a subsidiary of Haights Cross Communications Company.

A Haights Cross Communications ✦ Company

Copyright © 2004 by Chelsea House Publishers. All rights reserved. No part of this publication may be reproduced or transmitted in any form or by any means without the written permission of the publisher.

The Chelsea House World Wide Web address is
www.chelseahouse.com

Printed and bound in the United States of America.

9 8 7 6 5 4 3 2 1

Library of Congress Cataloging-in-Publication Data
Sonneborn, Liz.
  The Star-Spangled Banner : the story behind our national anthem / by Liz Sonneborn.
    p. cm. — (America in words and song)
Summary: Describes the events that led Francis Scott Key to write "The Star-Spangled Banner" and discusses the meaning of the song and its importance as the national anthem of the United States.
Includes bibliographical references and index.
  ISBN 0-7910-7337-8
1. Baltimore, Battle of, Baltimore, Md., 1814—Juvenile literature. 2. United States—History—War of 1812—Flags—Juvenile literature. 3. Flags—United States—History—19th century—Juvenile literature. 4. Key, Francis Scott, 1779–1843—Juvenile literature. 5. Star-spangled banner (Song)—Juvenile literature. [1. Baltimore, Battle of, Baltimore, Md., 1814. 2. United States—History—War of 1812. 3. Flags—United States. 4. Key, Francis Scott, 1779–1843. 5. Star-spangled banner (Song)] I. Title. II. Series.
  E356.B2S65 2004
  929.9'2'0973—dc21   2003004046

Selected Sources

Chambers, John W., III. *The Oxford Companion to American Military History*. New York: Oxford University Press, 1998.

Molotsky, Irvin. *The Flag, the Poet and the Song: The Story of the Star-Spangled Banner*. New York: Dutton, 2001.

The Smithsonian's Star-Spangled Banner Web Site: *americanhistory.si.edu/ssb*

Taylor, Lonn. *The Star-Spangled Banner: The Flag That Inspired the National Anthem*. New York: Harry N. Abrams, 2000.

Editorial Credits

Colleen Sexton, editor; Takeshi Takahashi, designer; Mary Englar, photo researcher; Jennifer Krassy Peiler, layout

Content Reviewer

Abbi Wicklein-Bayne, The Star-Spangled Banner Flag House, Baltimore, Maryland

Photo Credits

Bettman/Corbis: cover (Francis Scott Key), 12–13, 14, 15, 23; Maryland Historical Society, Baltimore, MD: cover (sheet music), 16, 17, 18, 19; Library of Congress: title page, 20, 24, 25, 26 (right); Reuters NewMedia Inc./Corbis: 4, 5; North Wind Picture Archive: 6, 7, 8, 9; Gallon Historical Art, www.gallon.com: 10; AFP/Corbis: 11, 30; Corbis: 26 (left); James Marshall/Corbis: 27

Table of Contents

Introduction

On the morning of December 11, 2001, the first notes of a single song rang out across the nation. At state capitols, city halls, schools, and military bases, Americans came together to sing "The Star-Spangled Banner." Most had learned the song's words when they were small children. Then, these **lyrics** probably had little meaning. But now they helped the singers express both grief and hope at a troubled time. As if with one voice, millions of Americans sang, "O say can you see...."

The occasion was the three-month anniversary of the September 11 terrorist attacks. On that day, terrorists hijacked two airplanes and flew them into the World Trade Center in New York City. They steered another plane into the Pentagon in Washington, D.C. A fourth hijacked plane crashed into a field in Pennsylvania. In all, the terrorists killed nearly 3,000 people. "The Star-Spangled Banner" was chosen to honor those lost on that terrible September day.

Members of the U.S. military hang a flag at the Pentagon in Washington, D.C., before a ceremony to mark the three-month anniversary of the September 11 terrorist attacks. During the ceremony, the crowd turned toward the flag and sang "The Star-Spangled Banner" to remember those who had died.

Fire fighters pause from their work at the wreckage of the World Trade Center to listen to "The Star-Spangled Banner" on December 11, 2001.

Probably few people singing remembered that the song's lyrics were written at another moment of crisis for America. The words were the work of poet Francis Scott Key. He wrote them 187 years earlier during the War of 1812 (1812–1815). At that time, the United States was also under attack by a foreign enemy. Then as now, Americans drew comfort from the moving words and rousing music of "The Star-Spangled Banner"—the song that became our national **anthem**.

"Not only is ['The Star-Spangled Banner'] part of our identity as Americans, it is also the song to whose tune the world has been saved time and time again throughout this century. Like the flag it celebrates, it ought to make us turn inward and contemplate everything America means to us."

—Concert pianist and political lecturer Balint Vazsonyi in *The National Review*, 1997

5

A Rescue Mission

During the War of 1812, the British sailed up Chesapeake Bay on their way to attack Washington, D.C.

The story of "The Star-Spangled Banner" begins in August 1814. The United States and Britain were at war. They had been fighting over shipping rights on the high seas for more than a year. British troops had recently attacked Washington, D.C., setting fire to many important government buildings. Among them were the White House and the U.S. Capitol.

British forces left Washington, D.C., in late August. They marched northeastward toward Baltimore, then the third largest city in the United States. Baltimore was also a center for shipping and shipbuilding. If the British could take Baltimore, they could destroy many American ships. Without ships, the United States would have little hope of winning the war.

While trudging through the Maryland countryside, some British soldiers raided American farms and houses. One group broke into Academy Hill, the beautiful home of a well-known doctor named William Beanes. The soldiers were looking for food, drink, and any valuable items they could carry away. But Beanes and his friends were able to round up the British thieves and place them under arrest. One soldier, however, managed to escape. He reached the British army commander, General Robert Ross, and told him what had happened. Ross then sent troops to arrest Beanes.

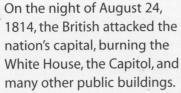

On the night of August 24, 1814, the British attacked the nation's capital, burning the White House, the Capitol, and many other public buildings.

The soldiers jailed Beanes in General Ross's warship, the *Tonnant*. Although Beanes was an American, his captors believed he was British. Saying he was disloyal to Britain, they charged Beanes with **treason** and threatened to hang him.

Francis Scott Key, a well-respected lawyer from Georgetown, soon heard about his friend's capture. Key went to see President James Madison right away. The president gave Key permission to negotiate with the British on Beanes's behalf. He also asked that Colonel John Skinner accompany Key. Skinner was an expert in arranging the release of war prisoners.

Francis Scott Key

Born in 1779, Francis Scott Key grew up in a wealthy Maryland family. He attended St. John's College and then opened a successful law practice. In his free time, he wrote poetry. Key rose to fame after writing the words to "The Star-Spangled Banner" in 1814. Poetry, however, remained just a hobby for Key. He continued to practice law. From 1833 to 1841, he served as U.S. district attorney for Washington, D.C. While at this job, he argued several cases before the U.S. Supreme Court. Key died in 1843. Fourteen years later, a collection of his poetry was published.

Francis Scott Key

The two men set off on September 3, riding quickly by horseback to Baltimore's Fort McHenry. From there, they set sail in a small boat in search of the *Tonnant*. After two days of sailing, Key and Skinner sighted the ship in Chesapeake Bay. They flew a white flag to show they came in peace. The British allowed the two men to board their warship.

Key and Skinner pleaded their case to General Ross. They showed him letters from British soldiers who had been wounded. Dr. Beanes had treated the men, and they wrote about his kindness. Ross agreed to let Beanes go, but not until after his forces attacked Baltimore. Key and Skinner would also have to stay until after the battle. Ross feared they would leak British battle plans to the U.S. Army. He sent the three men back to their small boat, which was now tied to another British warship. While the British prepared for battle, all the three Americans could do was watch and wait.

From 1793 to 1814, France and Britain were at war. While these two countries battled, the United States was able to take over much of the sea trade in Europe. But in 1806, the British started to set up blockades that kept U.S. trading ships from reaching French ports. Ships had to pay a fee to pass through the British blockades. In turn, France warned U.S. trading ships not to stop at the British blockades on their way to France. If they stopped, the French would later seize the U.S. ships. Many American traders had to stop sailing to British and French ports.

U.S. sea traders faced a second challenge from Britain. British sailors started boarding American ships and taking their crews hostage. The American sailors were then forced to work on British ships. The British took about 6,000 American sailors by force.

Britain's actions made sea trading nearly impossible for the United States. On June 1, 1812, President James Madison asked Congress to declare war on Britain. The War of 1812 was waged on both land and sea. Soldiers fought battles in the United States and in Canada, which was then ruled by Britain. By 1814, Britain had defeated France and was tired of war. Britain and the United States agreed to end the war by signing the Treaty of Ghent in Belgium on December 24, 1814. The treaty became official on February 17, 1815.

Seeking men to serve in their navy, British officers boarded American trading ships and took their crews by force.

9

The Perilous Fight

From his boat, Key could spy star-shaped Fort McHenry several miles in the distance. The U.S. Army had built the fort to protect Baltimore from a sea attack. Major George Armistead was the commander at Fort McHenry. A year earlier, Armistead had hired flag maker Mary Pickersgill to sew a huge American flag to fly over the fort. At the time, he had told his own commander that Fort McHenry needed "a flag so large that the British will have no difficulty in seeing it from a distance."

Fort McHenry guarded the waters of the Patapsco River, which leads to the city of Baltimore.

When U.S. Navy officers needed a flag for Fort McHenry, they called on Mary Pickersgill. She was one of Baltimore's best flag makers. Pickersgill had help from her mother, Rebecca Young, her daughter, and two nieces. They worked on the flag for six weeks starting in July 1813. They sewed a huge flag, measuring 30 feet (9 meters) tall by 42 feet (13 meters) wide. It had 15 stars and 15 stripes, which was the official U.S. flag design at that time.

After the War of 1812, the fort's commander, Major George Armistead, took home the flag as a keepsake. Many historians believe it was his wife who sewed a large "A" on the flag to stand for the family name. On the flag, it looks like an upside-down "V." Over the years, people took or were given small pieces of the flag as remembrances. This tradition was called "souveniring." In this way, the flag was whittled down to its present size of 30 feet (9 meters) tall by 33 feet (10 meters) wide.

Today, the flag is known as the Star-Spangled Banner. It can be seen at the National Museum of American History in Washington, D.C. Over time, the flag's wool and cotton fabric has weakened. In 1999, the museum started a project to preserve the flag. Once completed, it will become part of a special display at the museum.

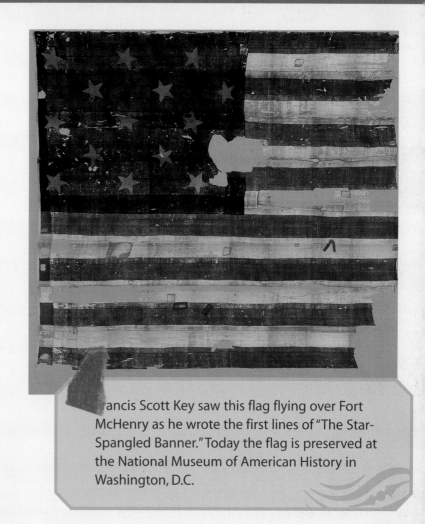

Francis Scott Key saw this flag flying over Fort McHenry as he wrote the first lines of "The Star-Spangled Banner." Today the flag is preserved at the National Museum of American History in Washington, D.C.

The soldiers at Fort McHenry now scrambled to prepare for battle. They knew about the British attack on Washington, D.C. From Baltimore, they had seen the flames of the burning U.S. Capitol. The soldiers were determined that Baltimore would not meet the same fate.

At dawn on September 13, 1814, the battle began. With bombs raining down, Key grew anxious. He paced back and forth in his boat, watching as hundreds of explosions lit the sky. Key later described the horrible sight: "The heavens aglow were a seething sea of flame, and the waters of the harbor, lashed into an angry sea by vibrations."

By afternoon, the air was filled with smoke and rain. The haze made it impossible to see what was happening. But as he heard the terrifying whooshing sounds of the British bombs, Key began to fear the worst.

From their ships on the Patapsco River, the British fired bombs, rockets, and cannon shells at Fort McHenry, filling the air with thick smoke.

Unknown to Key, the battle was actually going badly for the British. They had underestimated the American forces. The 1,000 U.S. soldiers at the fort held off the British with large naval guns. Quick-thinking American officers had also sunk more than 20 ships in Baltimore Harbor before the battle. The sunken ships created an underwater wall that kept the British ships too far away to seriously damage the fort. In addition, about 15,000 volunteers had joined a **militia** to help defend Baltimore.

This large force prevented British troops from attacking the city by land.

Throughout the night, British forces continued to **shell** Fort McHenry. British soldiers fired off more than 1,500 bombs. Then, at about 7:00 the next morning, the thunder of explosions stopped. The sudden silence was almost unbearable for Key and his companions. The sky was dark and clouded with smoke. They stared toward the fort, waiting for a sign of who had won the great battle.

Traveling by ship, General Robert Ross landed his troops near Baltimore and led them in the ground attack on the city. But a single shot took his life, leaving British soldiers shaken by the death of one of their greatest military leaders.

The Storm Flag

It was raining during much of the Battle of Baltimore. Fort McHenry didn't fly its best flags during bad weather. Instead, soldiers put up a smaller flag made by Mary Pickersgill called a "storm flag." But when the rain stopped and the battle was won, they raised the huge Star-Spangled Banner in victory. This great flag is the one Francis Scott Key saw when the smoke of battle cleared.

Key lifted a small telescope to his eye. Finally, as dawn broke, a shaft of gold light streaked across the sky. It fell on the fort, lighting up the huge American flag flying above it. Seeing the stars and stripes, Key felt a wave of relief. It was proof that the Americans had defeated the powerful British. Baltimore was safe.

Filled with emotion, Key pulled a letter from his pocket. On the back, he started writing a poem. It began, "O say can you see…"

When Francis Scott Key saw the American flag waving above Fort McHenry, he knew the British had failed to take Baltimore.

A Patriotic Song

True to their word, the British freed Key, Skinner, and Beanes after the battle. As the group sailed to Baltimore on September 16, Key worked on his poem about the American victory. That night he stayed at the Indian Queen Inn in Baltimore. There, he studied the words he had scribbled after the battle. From his notes, Key drafted the first eight lines of his poem and then three more eight-line **stanzas**.

Pleased with his work, Key showed the poem to his brother-in-law Joseph Nicholson. Nicholson had been the second-in-command at Fort McHenry. Key told him that even "if it had been a hanging matter to make that poem, I must have made it."

This is the earliest known draft of the poem written by Francis Scott Key. A printer used this manuscript to set the poem in type for the first time.

On September 17, 1814, someone—perhaps Nicholson—took the poem to a printer. The printer's assistant, Samuel Sands, set it in type as a **broadside**—a handbill printed on only one side. On the broadside, the poem was titled "The Defence of Fort McHenry." Later, Key renamed it "The Star-Spangled Banner" after a line in the first stanza.

A stack of broadsides was taken to Fort McHenry. The soldiers there all rushed to get a copy. The people of Baltimore were also eager to read the poem. Within days, the city's newspaper, *The Baltimore Patriot*, had printed Key's work. Actors began reciting the poem in the city's theaters. Outside Baltimore, the public was just as enthusiastic. By mid-October, the poem had appeared in 17 newspapers in the eastern United States.

Key's poem was first printed as a broadside and titled "The Defence of Fort McHenry."

DEFENCE OF FORT M'HENRY.

The annexed song was composed under the following circumstances—A gentleman had left Baltimore, in a flag of truce for the purpose of getting released from the British fleet, a friend of his who had been captured at Marlborough.—He went as far as the mouth of the Patuxent, and was not permitted to return lest the intended attack on Baltimore should be disclosed. He was therefore brought up the Bay to the mouth of the Patapsco, where the flag vessel was kept under the guns of a frigate, and he was compelled to witness the bombardment of Fort M'Henry, which the Admiral had boasted that he would carry in a few hours, and that the city must fall. He watched the flag at the Fort through the whole day with an anxiety that can be better felt than described, until the night prevented him from seeing it. In the night he watched the Bomb Shells, and at early dawn his eye was again greeted by the proudly waving flag of his country.

Tune—Anacreon in Heaven.

O ! say can you see by the dawn's early light,
　What so proudly we hailed at the twilight's last gleaming,
Whose broad stripes and bright stars through the perilous fight,
　O'er the ramparts we watch'd, were so gallantly streaming?
And the Rockets' red glare, the Bombs bursting in air,
Gave proof through the night that our Flag was still there;
　　O ! say does that star-spangled Banner yet wave,
　　O'er the Land of the free, and the home of the brave?

On the shore dimly seen through the mists of the deep,
　Where the foe's haughty host in dread silence reposes,
What is that which the breeze, o'er the towering steep,
　As it fitfully blows, half conceals, half discloses?
Now it catches the gleam of the morning's first beam,
In full glory reflected now shines in the stream,
　　'Tis the star spangled banner, O ! long may it wave
　　O'er the land of the free and the home of the brave.

And where is that band who so vauntingly swore
　That the havoc of war and the battle's confusion,
A home and a country, shall leave us no more ?
　Their blood has washed out their foul footsteps pollution.
No refuge could save the hireling and slave,
From the terror of flight or the gloom of the grave,
　　And the star-spangled banner in triumph doth wave,
　　O'er the Land of the Free, and the Home of the Brave.

O ! thus be it ever when freemen shall stand,
　Between their lov'd home, and the war's desolation,
Blest with vict'ry and peace, may the Heav'n rescued land,
　Praise the Power that hath made and preserv'd us a nation!
Then conquer we must, when our cause it is just,
And this be our motto—" In God is our Trust ;"
　　And the star-spangled Banner in triumph shall wave,
　　O'er the Land of the Free, and the Home of the Brave.

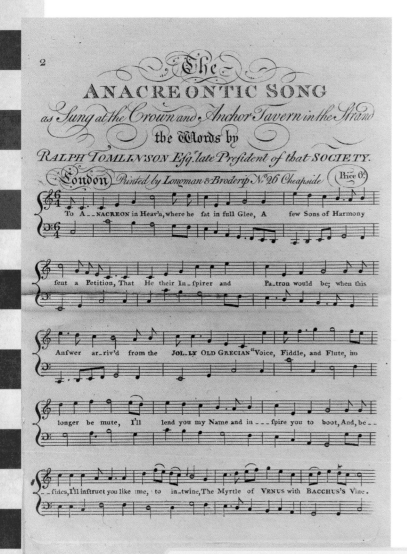

In November, Thomas Carr, a music publisher, printed the poem as sheet music. It was titled "The Star Spangled Banner: A Patriotic Song." Key's poem was put to the tune "To Anacreon in Heaven." This song was about a Greek poet named Anacreon who lived more than 2,500 years ago. It is most likely that Englishman John Stafford Smith composed the song in 1777 for the Anacreontic Society. This gentlemen's club gathered several times a year to listen to music and sing. By the early 1800s, "To Anacreon in Heaven" was a popular song in the taverns of both Britain and the United States. Songbooks included more than 85 versions of the lyrics to go with the tune. Key probably wrote his poem with the song in mind.

This song sheet shows some of the words and music for "To Anacreon in Heaven," a popular tune that was paired with Francis Scott Key's poem in November 1814.

"The Star-Spangled Banner" quickly became one of America's favorite **patriotic** anthems. At political meetings, bands often played the popular tune. At social gatherings, citizens sang Key's words to show their loyalty to their country. In 1843, an article in the *Baltimore American* declared, "so long as patriotism dwells among us, so long will this song be the theme of our nation."

In 1854, when this sheet music for "The Star-Spangled Banner" was published, the song was still one of America's favorite patriotic tunes.

The Meaning Behind the Song

This sheet music contained four popular national songs of the 1800s, including "The Star-Spangled Banner."

It is hardly surprising that Americans of Key's day welcomed "The Star-Spangled Banner." His words told the story of an exciting sea battle. They also celebrated a great military upset on land, one that filled all Americans with pride. Few would have predicted that the untrained Maryland militia would successfully defend Baltimore from the mighty British Army.

"The Star-Spangled Banner" also stirred in Americans a new sense of patriotism. When Key wrote his poem, the United States was still a young nation. Just some 40 years earlier, Americans were subjects of the British king. They established an independent country only after defeating Britain in the Revolutionary War (1775–1783). Even after the **revolution**, the British did not treat the United States as a free country. Their lack of respect toward America helped lead to the War of 1812.

The fighting ended in early 1815, just months after the Battle of Baltimore. Neither the United States nor Britain could claim a total victory. But for Americans, the war's end was a turning point. They had defended their freedom against the British, not once, but twice. The people of the United States now felt sure their country would last.

The Star-Spangled Banner

This version of "The Star-Spangled Banner" is from Francis Scott Key's original manuscript:

O say can you see, by the dawn's early light,
What so proudly we hail'd at the twilight's last gleaming,
Whose broad stripes and bright stars through the perilous fight
O'er the ramparts we watch'd were so gallantly streaming?
And the rocket's red glare, the bomb bursting in air,
Gave proof through the night that our flag was still there,
O say does that star-spangled banner yet wave
O'er the land of the free and the home of the brave?

On the shore dimly seen through the mists of the deep
Where the foe's haughty host in dread silence reposes,
What is that which the breeze, o'er the towering steep,
As it fitfully blows, half conceals, half discloses?
Now it catches the gleam of the morning's first beam,
In full glory reflected now shines in the stream,
'Tis the star-spangled banner — O long may it wave
O'er the land of the free and the home of the brave!

And where is that band who so vauntingly swore,
That the havoc of war and the battle's confusion
A home and a Country should leave us no more?
Their blood has wash'd out their foul footstep's pollution.
No refuge could save the hireling and slave
From the terror of flight or the gloom of the grave,
And the star-spangled banner in triumph doth wave
O'er the land of the free and the home of the brave.

O thus be it ever when freemen shall stand
Between their lov'd home and the war's desolation!
Blest with vict'ry and peace may the heav'n rescued land
Praise the power that hath made and preserv'd us a nation!
Then conquer we must, when our cause it is just,
And this be our motto — "In God is our trust,"
And the star-spangled banner in triumph shall wave
O'er the land of the free and the home of the brave.

What Do the Words Mean?

desolation: damage and ruin

fitfully: irregularly; from time to time

gallantly: grandly

gleaming: flash or beam of light

haughty: very proud

havoc: damage and ruin

hireling: a person who performs work only for money

o'er: a shortcut for the word "over"

perilous: dangerous

ramparts: barriers built to protect against attack

reposes: lies in rest

star-spangled: sprinkled with stars

steep: a sharp slope

thro': a shortcut for the word "through"

vauntingly: boastfully

"The Star-Spangled Banner" put this newfound confidence into song. When Americans sang the words, they saw the star-spangled banner Key described as a **symbol** of their country. Just like the Fort McHenry flag, their nation would endure.

In the first verse of the song, Key poses a question. It was the same question he asked himself as the Battle of Baltimore came to an end: Is the American flag still flying over Fort McHenry?

"'The Star-Spangled Banner' is today the anthem of a free people. For American soldiers, scattered in every corner of the earth, nothing expresses better the people's will to end oppression than the stirring words of this song."

—From *Songs of Many Wars,* 1943

The first two lines ask, "can you see, by the dawn's early light" the flag Key and his companions had saluted the night before ("What so proudly we hail'd at the twilight's last gleaming"). Key then describes how the flag, with its "broad stripes and bright stars" had been waving ("gallantly streaming"). In the fifth and sixth lines, Key adds that the light of the British bombs ("the rocket's red glare") showed him during the night that the flag was still flying. At the end of the verse, Key repeats his central question: "O say does that star-spangled banner yet wave/O'er the land of the free and the home of the brave?"

Key reveals the answer to his question in the song's second verse. First, he watches an object that "fitfully blows" in the breeze. Then, at the first light of dawn ("the gleam of the morning's first beam"), he finally sees that it is, in fact, the flag: "Tis the star-spangled banner—O long may it wave."

The flag that inspired "The Star-Spangled Banner" was displayed at the Boston Navy Yard in 1874. This is the earliest known photograph of the flag.

In the song's third verse, Key turns his attention to the British enemy. At the battle's end, he asks, where are the British soldiers? He then explains that they have all retreated ("the terror of flight") or died in battle ("the gloom of the grave"). Key also takes the opportunity to insult the British soldiers, calling them "hireling[s] and slave[s]."

Key uses his fourth verse to celebrate the American victory. He holds that God has been on the Americans' side, blessing the United States ("the heav'n rescued land") "with vict'ry and peace." Key calls on all "freemen" to praise God ("Praise the power that hath made and preserv'd us a nation!"). In the poem's final lines, Key declares that with God's help, the United States will always survive and prosper: "And this be our motto—'In God is our trust,'/And the star-spangled banner in triumph shall wave / O'er the land of the free and the home of the brave."

Our National Anthem

Long after most Americans had forgotten the Battle of Baltimore, they continued to sing "The Star-Spangled Banner." The song was especially popular during wartime. In the mid-1800s, the Northern states battled the Southern states in the U.S. Civil War (1861–1865). Both armies sang "The Star-Spangled Banner" as they marched. Americans again embraced the song during World War I (1914–1918). Starting in 1916, President Woodrow Wilson ordered "The Star-Spangled Banner" to be played during certain government occasions.

This 1861 sheet music for "The Star-Spangled Banner" shows a Union soldier holding the American flag. The song was popular with both Union and Confederate troops during the Civil War.

On Memorial Day 1943, a crowd at Arlington National Cemetery in Virginia stood to sing "The Star-Spangled Banner" in honor of the soldiers buried there.

"The Star-Spangled Banner" was inspiring to Americans. It had seen them through the dark days of war and helped them celebrate the nation's victories. Many Americans wanted the song to become the country's national anthem. A national anthem is the official patriotic song of a country. It is played or sung at public functions—from government receptions to sporting events.

The U.S. Congress first considered making "The Star-Spangled Banner" the national anthem in 1912. During the next 19 years, Congress was presented with more than 40 **bills** on the matter. None, however, were passed into law. Too many citizens and members of Congress thought the song was a bad choice for the national anthem.

Newly sworn-in American citizens showed their love for their new country by singing the national anthem in the 1940s.

Some people felt "The Star-Spangled Banner" was too hard to sing. They said an average singer might be able to hit the high notes or the low notes, but not both. Others objected to the song because the tune was English. They believed that both the music and words of a true national anthem should be written by Americans. Still others felt "The Star-Spangled Banner" wasn't the right choice because it told the story of a

In 1951, during the Korean War, American soldiers at a memorial service sang "The Star-Spangled Banner" to honor fellow soldiers who had died in battle.

battle. Among them was music professor Peter W. Dykem. In 1930, he argued that "the national anthem must be sung even when there is no crisis. 'The Star-Spangled Banner' is an occasional song....When it is not sung on an occasion of national stress, like a declaration of war, it falls flat."

Despite these views, the United States finally adopted "The Star-Spangled Banner" as its national anthem on March 3, 1931. Occasionally, someone still complains that the tune is hard to sing and the words are hard to remember. But most Americans have great affection for our national anthem. It says that Americans will never give up. They will overcome challenges and endure. And in both times of joy and times of sorrow, "The Star-Spangled Banner" reminds Americans of the love they share for the "land of the free and the home of the brave."

A boy stands with a baseball player to sing the national anthem before the first pitch of a game.

July 1814

British troops invade Washington, D.C.

September 13–14, 1814

The British attack Fort McHenry; Key begins writing the poem "The Defence of Fort McHenry."

September 17, 1814

Key's poem is printed as a broadside.

November 1814

Sheet music titled "The Star-Spangled Banner: A Patriotic Song" is published, pairing Key's poem with the tune "To Anacreon in Heaven."

August 1,1779

Francis Scott Key is born in Maryland.

1840

1820

1800

1780

June 18, 1812

The United States declares war on Britain.

July–August 1813

Flag maker Mary Pickersgill sews a huge American flag for Fort McHenry in Baltimore.

1912

The U.S. Congress first considers a bill proposing "The Star-Spangled Banner" as the official national anthem.

1916

President Woodrow Wilson orders "The Star-Spangled Banner" to be played at official government events.

March 4, 1931

President Herbert Hoover signs a law making "The Star-Spangled Banner" the national anthem.

1999

The National Museum of American History in Washington, D.C., begins a project to preserve the Star-Spangled Banner flag.

1900 1920 1940 1960 1980 2000

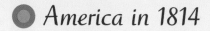

America in 1814

Francis Scott Key wrote "The Star-Spangled Banner" in 1814. What was happening in the United States that year?

★ The United States is made up of 18 states.

★ Six million people live in the United States.

★ The president is James Madison.

★ The country is fighting the War of 1812 against Britain.

★ U.S. troops led by General Andrew Jackson fight and defeat the Creek Indian Nation.

★ The British burn the Library of Congress during their attack on Washington, D.C.; later, the U.S. government buys Thomas Jefferson's library of nearly 7,000 volumes to replace the books that were destroyed.

★ Francis Cabot Lowell builds a textile factory in Waltham, Massachusetts, marking the beginning of the American Industrial Revolution.

★ The United States and Britain sign the Treaty of Ghent, officially ending the War of 1812.

Glossary

anthem (AN-thuhm) a patriotic song; a national anthem is a country's official patriotic song.

bill (BIL) a written plan for a new law that is sent to Congress to be debated

broadside (BRAWD-side) a large sheet of paper usually printed on one side

lyrics (LEER-iks) words set to music

militia (muh-LISH-uh) a group of citizens who volunteer to fight when they are needed

patriotic (pay-tree-AH-tik) having love for your country

revolution (rev-uh-LOO-shuhn) a violent uprising by the people of a country that changes its government

shell (SHEL) to fire small bombs from a cannon

stanza (STAN-zuh) a group of lines in a poem or song

symbol (SIM-buhl) an object that stands for something else

treason (TREE-zuhn) the crime of betraying one's country

At the 2000 Olympics in Sydney, Australia, the U.S. national anthem played at the women's basketball medal ceremony. The U.S. team (in white) took home the gold medal.

To Learn More

READ THESE BOOKS

Bowdish, Lynea. *Francis Scott Key and "The Star-Spangled Banner."* New York: Mondo, 2002.

Britton, Tamara L. *The American Flag*. Edina, Minn.: Abdo, 2003.

Gregson, Susan R. *Francis Scott Key: Patriotic Poet.* Mankato, Minn.: Bridgestone Books, 2003.

Kroll, Steven. *By the Dawn's Early Light: The Story of the Star-Spangled Banner*. New York: Scholastic, 1994.

Maynard, Charles W. *Fort McHenry*. New York: Rosen, 2002.

Quiri, Patricia Ryon. *The National Anthem.* New York: Children's Press, 1998.

Stefoff, Rebecca. *The War of 1812*. Tarrytown, N.Y.: Benchmark Books, 2001.

LOOK UP THESE INTERNET SITES

The Star-Spangled Banner Flag House
www.flaghouse.org
Learn more about Mary Pickersgill, the woman who sewed the Star-Spangled Banner flag.

Fort McHenry National Monument and Historic Shrine
www.bcpl.net/~etowner/patriots.html
Take a virtual tour of Fort McHenry and learn more about this birthplace of "The Star-Spangled Banner."

The Star-Spangled Banner
americanhistory.si.edu/ssb
Find out more about the flag that inspired Francis Scott Key's famous poem.

The Star-Spangled Banner Project
www.historychannel.com/starspangled_archive/home.html
Discover a wealth of information about "The Star-Spangled Banner," including a quiz and a history of the American flag.

INTERNET SEARCH KEY WORDS
Star-Spangled Banner, War of 1812, Francis Scott Key, Fort McHenry, Mary Pickersgill, national anthem

Index

1067764900